at **work**

ADRIAN FURNHAM

**Adrian Furnham** is an academic, consultant, writer and broadcaster. A professor of psychology at the University of London, he previously lectured in psychology at Oxford University and is the author of 30 books and over 400 articles on psychology-related topics. He is a chartered occupational psychologist and makes frequent contributions

**Management Shapers** is a comprehensive series covering all the crucial management skill areas. Each book includes the key issues, helpful starting points and practical advice in a concise and lively style. Together, they form an accessible library reflecting current best practice – ideal for study or quick reference.

The Chartered Institute of Personnel and Development is the leading publisher of books and reports for personnel and training professionals, students, and all those concerned with the effective management and development of people at work. For full details of all our titles, please contact the Publishing Department:
*tel.* 020-8263 3387
*fax* 020-8263 3850
*e-mail* publish@cipd.co.uk
The catalogue of all CIPD titles can be viewed on the CIPD website:
www.cipd.co.uk/publications

# body language at work

## ADRIAN FURNHAM

CHARTERED INSTITUTE OF PERSONNEL AND DEVELOPMENT

Design by Curve
Typesetting by Paperweight
Printed in Great Britain by
The Guernsey Press, Channel Islands

*British Library Cataloguing in Publication Data*
A catalogue record for this book is available from the
British Library

ISBN
0-85292-771-1

The views expressed in this book are the author's own and
may not necessarily reflect those of the CIPD.

Chartered Institute of Personnel and Development, CIPD House,
Camp Road, London SW19 4UX
Tel.: 020 8971 9000   Fax: 020 8263 3333
E-mail: cipd@cipd.co.uk   Website: www.cipd.co.uk
Incorporated by Royal Charter. Registered charity no. 1079797

# contents

**For Benedict**
Wink, Wink; Nod, Nod...Know what I mean?

# Other titles in the series:

# 1 bodily communication

## What is body language?

Bodily communication is communication without words: it is anything someone does to which someone else assigns meaning. It may be structured (following certain rules) but is more likely to be unstructured; it may be continuous, unlike language, which comes in disconnected units; it may be learnt but parts seem innate; and it may be 'right-' as opposed to 'left-brained'.

It is no wonder that so many people are fascinated by body language. We are all 'manwatchers' and amateur psychologists, partly because we have to be. In every aspect of communication at work – the selection interview, the annual appraisal, the board meeting – we need to observe others carefully to try to understand better what they are feeling as well as (really) saying. Being adults, we are all skilful deceivers; we have learnt, for myriad reasons, to present ourselves in a particular way; to manage the impression we leave; not always to say directly what we mean (perhaps to protect others' feelings); to sell products or ideas; and to explain away some undesirable behaviour.

As a result, many people believe messages conveyed by different body signals, particularly emotional states and attitudes to oneself and others, are somehow more real, more fundamental. We send and 'leak' non-verbal signals which may or may not be 'picked up' in the communication process. The sender of the message may be aware or unaware of the signals he or she sends. Indeed, receivers may not always be aware of the messages they are actually picking up. For instance, most people are not aware of their pupil dilations; nor are observers aware that they can on specific occasions respond positively to dilated pupils (when people are sexually aroused).

Body language can be subtle or blatant; it can be consciously sent and unconsciously received; it can be carefully practised and displayed but also physiologically uncontrollable; it can 'let you down' by revealing your true beliefs and behaviours, but also (when learnt) help enormously to put across a message. Facial expressions, gestures, head and gaze movements, body contact and orientation, sheer physical proximity as well as tone of voice, clothes and body adornments send clear messages ... some even intended!

Consider the ability of actors on the silent screen (Chaplin, Keaton, Lloyd) to communicate. They have had to be perceptive students of expression. They use sign language (gestures to replace words, numbers and punctuation marks) to convey a bewildering array of meanings.

Non-verbal communication is a more primitive and powerful means of communication than verbal communication. Some things may be better expressed non-verbally than verbally (pain, shape of rooms). Subtle and intentionally vague messages can also be sent through the imprecise channel of non-verbal communication. Cultures develop specific rules about non-verbal communication, often set out in etiquette books, such as when, where and why to touch others, how to give greetings etc.

Non-verbal communication is a rather misleading term. 'Non-verbal' excludes vocal or paralinguistic cues and signals like emotional tone of speech, which is clearly very important. Body language also excludes vocal cues. 'Communication' suggests furthermore that giver and sender (encoder and decoder) are conscious speakers of the same body language! Intentional messages may or may not be intentionally received non-verbally. Equally, unintentional messages may be unintentionally sent and received.

## The function of body language

Non-verbal messages are used to replace, reinforce and occasionally contradict a verbal message. Non-verbal cues can easily substitute for verbal cues: for instance 'Yes/No' or 'I don't know.' Often non-verbal cues can stress, underline or exaggerate the meaning of the verbal message. But non-verbal cues can also contradict verbal cues. A 'kinetic slip' is a contradictory signal where words give one message, voice and expression another. 'I am telling you I am not angry' or 'Of course it did not upset me' can be easily said in one of two ways.

Bodily communication complements and contradicts speech. One can non-verbally restate a message so as, in effect, to repeat it. A non-verbal signal can substitute for a verbal message or indeed accentuate it. Most obviously, non-verbal communication serves to regulate or co-ordinate daily dialogue between people. It is through non-verbal cues that we know when it is our turn to talk and when the topic of conversation is becoming embarrassing; certain things are deliberately not said or coded in polite language.

### Body communication as metaphor

People appear to see non-verbal behaviour metaphorically. Thus people use the *approach or distance* metaphor, which suggests that chosen location/distance is an indication of liking or closeness. Physical proximity implies mental closeness, alliance or liking, as all children instinctively know. The *excitement or arousal* metaphor suggests that facial expression, speech rate and speed of movement are indications of excitement and that all non-verbal behaviour gives some insight into how interested, involved and excited a person is. The *power* metaphor emphasises that non-verbal communication tells us about dominance and submission in everyday communication. Powerful people are 'allowed to' engage in more eye contact than less powerful people – and all children know this, too. Put simply, body language tells one about the closeness, relative excitement and status of two or more people communicating with each other.

## Sense and nonsense about body language

The first scientists to do a systematic study of body language were biologists. It is no surprise that those skilled in bird-watching were easily able to turn their skills to man-watching. Charles Darwin wrote the first acknowledged text in 1873, entitled *The Expression of the Emotions in Man and Animals*. Irenäus Eibl-Eibesfeldt (1971) wrote a scholarly popular biology book entitled *Love and Hate: Natural history of behavior patterns*. But it was Desmond Morris' book *The Naked Ape* – published in 1967, 94 years after Darwin – that electrified popular interest in body-watching.

For the last 30 years scientists from different disciplines – anthropology, psychology, sociology and zoology – have all brought their methods and concepts to bear in order to help in the understanding of bodily communication. More recently, physiologists, endocrinologists and sexologists have taken a particular interest in highly specific physiological processes that have non-verbal consequences.

Despite the excellent and careful research in the area, much nonsense still is written about the topic, often by journalists and other self-appointed 'experts' whose aim is to entertain rather than to enlighten. Non-verbal communication is too important to be ignored or misrepresented.

Fascination with the topic, as well as its obvious importance in business, has led many self-styled experts and gurus to make confident proclamations about non-verbal communication. Inevitably nearly all of their 'findings' and 'recommendations' over-emphasise the importance and power of non-verbal communication. Often there is no evidence whatsoever that the findings are true; although many exaggerate something that is based on fact. Misleading and sometimes completely incorrect statements about body language communication seem to fall into various areas:

1   *Symbolism* (All body communication is symbolic expression)

People with a fondness for psychoanalytic (Freudian) ideas love to interpret explicit behaviours as manifestations of (often unconscious) desires and behaviours. Thus one observer believed Prince Charles' habit of 'fiddling' with his cuff-links indicated that he felt chained by handcuffs to the monarchy. Those with a stiff and military bearing have 'imprisoned anxiety'. Numerous otherwise common behaviours like the wetting of lips, the crossing of legs, the folding of arms are all indicators of sexuality. The temptation of too many body language experts is that they favour a psychological over a more obvious explanation. It is too easy to over-interpret incorrectly. For instance, look at the table opposite and consider two types of explanation for the same behaviour (one innocent, the other not).

## *Body language: alternative interpretations*

| Behaviours | Psychological Explanation | Alternative Explanation |
|---|---|---|
| Hands in pockets | The person is secretive, withdrawn – possibly depressed. | It is cold. The person is searching for a small object. |
| Folded arms | Defensive act performed for physical reassurance. Indicator of uncertainty and lack of confidence. | It is cold; the arm-rests are occupied; it is comfortable. |
| Yawning | Faced with a difficult situation one would prefer to avoid. | Very tired. Not enough oxygen. |
| Crossed legs | Defensive, repressed, even feeling hostile. | Women are taught to cross legs to look more feminine; men do so because it is comfortable. |
| Nose-touching | The person is lying or covering up his or her emotions. | He or she has a cold or an itchy nose. |

2  *Power* (Bodily communication is always more powerful)

It is not uncommon to read statements like: 'Seventy per cent of the communicative power of a message is sent non-verbally' or 'It is not what you say but it is the way that you say it.' Body communication pundits have a natural inclination to 'talk up' their area of expertise, to over-emphasise its importance. Certainly non-verbal communication is often neglected in business, and paying attention to synchronising the verbal and the non-verbal cues is inevitably important.

Non-verbal communication can at times be extremely powerful – sheer rage or terror are often much more efficiently communicated through facial and body expression than through words. Pain or love can be communicated by those, such as children, who articulate their feelings through a limited vocabulary. But words have extraordinary precision. Further, if one uses gesture, for example, to communicate, it is immediately apparent that there are so few gestures compared to words. The power of bodily communication lies primarily in the fact that it often tells one about the physiological state of the individual because of changes in the central nervous system. But these physiological states are nearly always an expression of emotional extremes not that common in everyday life.

3   *Controllability* (We can control all the messages we send)

Some non-verbal behaviours, such as gestures and touch, are naturally controllable; others, such as sweating and pupil dilation, are not. Certainly, through relaxation techniques and fitness regimes one may attempt to influence the central nervous system, which is responsible for body signals. The skill is to be more aware of signals that are both sent and received. Most people in conversation are not particularly aware of others – or of their own legs and feet. They are not aware of small changes in posture and micro-facial expressions as certain things are said.

Once these behaviours have been witnessed on a video recording, it is surprisingly easy to see and understand their meaning. Once an 'actor' becomes an 'observer' of his or her own behaviour, awareness of what is going on is increased.

Naturally some people attempt to 'control' their non-verbal behaviour. Stage actors may be required to weep, rage or demonstrate fear, loathing or passion on cue. They have learnt, often with the help of make-up, to produce certain recognisable signals of those emotions. But most of us are not so gifted. Indeed, the more we try to control emotions – particularly if we try to conceal powerful emotions – the more they leak out non-verbally.

4   *You can read people like a book*

There are many misleading aspects to this analogy. Books are passive, other people are not. Most observers are aware that when two people are speaking, each is attempting to 'read' the other. The curious claim of many popular books is that it is possible simultaneously to read others but hide oneself – to hide or disguise one's secrets while putting on a believable front.

True experts in the area of non-verbal communication are surprisingly diffident on this point. Experts on lying point out how difficult it is to detect lying in the skilful dissimulator. They all point out how much information one needs to confirm an hypothesis that 'he is lying', 'she is an extrovert' or 'they are not competent in this area'.

Certainly, a knowledge of non-verbal communication and body language is very helpful in business. Understanding the motives, fears and strengths of those at selection committees or in bargaining situations is a considerable asset in the business world. Observing subtler movements in body language as it accompanies speech may be one of the best ways to gain advantage. And a knowledge of body language can also help one improve one's own performance at conferences, in appraisals and even in day-to-day management. One can rest assured that if such matters were not important, politicians, business people and diplomats would not spend so much money and time attending workshops on 'communication skills and body language'.

# 2 body signals: their nature and meaning

There are all sorts of ways of drawing up lists of the major body signals. In fact our everyday language shows how we note and understand different aspects of body language.

## Verbal language and body language

There are innumerable English phrases that seem to relate to body language. Consider the following:

- *Touch*: 'I touched her for a fiver.' 'I felt touched by his concern.' 'Her plight touched me.'
- *Posture*: When people are comfortable they usually balance their weight on both feet. Hence we have 'well-balanced', 'take a firm stand', 'know where you stand on this'. When uncomfortable, many people shift their weight from one foot to the other and can be seen to be 'shifty characters'.
- *Eye contact*: 'I see what you mean.' 'Seeing is believing.' 'I can't see any other solution.'
- *Gesture*: 'He gave me the cold shoulder.' This indicates that a person rejected what was being said and metaphorically turned away in disgust.
- *Territory/distance*: 'I feel close to him.' 'She is very stand-offish.' 'Back off from me, buster!' 'I prefer to keep her at arm's length.'
- *Orientation*: 'I dislike people who are always taking sides.' 'I feel diametrically opposed to everything he does.'

- □ *Odour*: 'I like the sweet smell of success.' 'He has a nose for where the money is.' 'Yet she still came up smelling of roses.' 'He is always sticking his nose in other people's business.' 'She always sticks her nose in the air.' 'I will ensure that I rub his nose in it.'
- △ *Body state expression*: Feeling is often expressed in terms of body language. Thus we: 'shoulder a burden', 'face up to issues', try to 'keep our chin up', 'grit our teeth' in the face of pain, have a 'stiff upper lip', 'bare our teeth' on occasion, 'catch the eye' of another, and 'shrug off' misfortune.

## Eye gaze

The eyes are indeed the messengers of the soul. We 'keep our eye in', 'have an eye to the main chance', 'keep our eyes open/peeled/skinned', 'see eye-to-eye with others' but 'turn a blind eye to certain events'. Some people are 'more than meets the eye'. Some individuals are the 'apple of one's eye', and others a 'sight for sore eyes'. You may prefer 'not to bat an eye' or to 'pull the wool over others' eyes'. And you can be 'up to your eyes' in trouble.

Where, when, and how we look are all part of the phenomenon of eye gaze, which is one of the most important and primitive ways of communication. Gaze plays a crucial role in conversation. Looking at another person is a way of getting feedback at particular points in the conversation. It is also used as a synchronising signal. People tend to look up at the end of utterances: this gives them feedback and gives their listeners warning that the speaker is about to stop talking. People also look up more at the end of grammatical breaks, but look away when hesitating, talking non-fluently or thinking. There is often mutual eye contact during attempted interruptions, laughing and when answering short questions. Gaze functions to encourage and persuade in all human beings. For instance we know:

- A looker may invite interaction by staring at another person who is on the other side of a room. The target's studied return of the gaze is generally interpreted as acceptance of the invitation, while averting the eyes is a rejection of the looker's request.

- There is more mutual eye contact between friends than others, and a looker's frank gaze is widely interpreted as positive regard.

- People who seek eye contact while speaking are regarded not only as exceptionally well-disposed by their targets, but also as more believable and earnest.

- If the usual short, intermittent gazes during conversation are replaced by gazes of longer duration, the target interprets this as meaning that the communication is less important than the personal relation between two people.

The amount of eye gaze imparts a great deal of information. Pupil dilation, blink rates, direction of gaze, widening of the eyes all send very clear messages. Consider the factors that determine the amount of eye gaze:

1 *Distance*: In lifts (elevators) we turn to face the door because we stand too close and reducing eye gaze helps to reduce the discomfort of having our body zones invaded.

2 *Topic of conversation*: It is no accident that Catholic confessionals and psychiatric couches are so arranged as to attempt to reduce the amount of contact between priest or therapist and the individual in the confessional or the patient in the room. When people are talking about shameful and embarrassing things or looking inward, it is better that they sense but do not see others, and that those listening do not (cannot) stare at them. People often find that they can have 'good conversations' walking or doing a co-operative activity, such as washing up, because they are close to, but not looking at, their companions. Intimate talk can be inhibited by eye contact.

3 *Attention*: Hitch hikers, charity-tin shakers and others all maximise eye contact to increase attention. People look at each other about 75 per cent of the time when talking but only 40 per cent of the time when listening. One looks to get, and keep, the attention of others.

4 *Interpersonal relationships*: People look at those they like more than those they do not like. Your pupils dilate more when you are looking at someone you like. Gaze also signals dominance: more powerful people are looked at

more (partly because they tend to look more and speak less). Threat is also indicated by gaze. Direct gaze signals threat, while cutting off or averting your gaze is likely to signal appeasement.

5   *Co-operation*: The extent to which people are willing to co-operate rather than compete is often communicated by gaze patterns. The amount and type of gaze is important. The common meaning of a high level of gaze is that the gazer is interested and attentive. However, combined with certain expressions it could as easily indicate threat.

6   *Personality*: Extroverts look more often, and for longer, at their interlocutors than introverts. Schizophrenics and depressed people tend to avert eye gaze.

Physiological changes in the eyes are most revealing. People who are angry or sexually aroused find that their pupils dilate. This is why women used to put 'belladonna' in their eyes to dilate the pupils. Unaware of why they found the woman attractive, men would often respond very positively to her enlarged pupils, which seemed to signal that she was sexually aroused and responsive. Women soon came to appreciate the special attention they received and hence the habit began.

People also disguise eye contact by wearing dark glasses or sunshades. Blind people do so to indicate their blindness but also because they cannot always 'face' a person. To avoid the embarrassment of not being able to 'look a person in the eye' when appropriate, blind people wear tinted glasses. Security people also wear dark glasses so that possible suspects cannot see the direction in which they are looking. Traffic police wear reflecting, mirrored glasses to reduce the possibility of an argument. Irate or nervous drivers can be put off a confrontation if they not only cannot see the eyes of the policeman but are also forced to see their own eyes. They experience *objective self-awareness*, seeing themselves as objects and not seeing those they are engaging in conversation.

Most of us know people who close their eyes while speaking. Such 'eye blocks' may occur because a person is bored or feels superior. They deny both speaker and listener the opportunity to receive and give feedback. Shy, introverted people also tend to have less open eye gaze.

## Facial expression

The face is a highly expressive region. The eyes, mouth and eyebrows are all able to move independently, allowing for many different expressions. The nose can be flared or wrinkled in a sneer. Skin colour, texture and moisture can give a great deal of information about an individual's mood and state of health. Simple line drawings of eyebrows, forehead and mouth in different expressions can send at least 10 emotional messages.

Certainly, many facial expressions – such as startled responses or expressions of pain – appear innate, rather than learnt or culturally variable. But there are cultural rules about appropriate expressions in various social settings. Thus one is expected to look cheerful at weddings, miserable at funerals, excited at sports matches.

People are known by their faces. People 'put on' faces and many believe that, after a time, one's face says a lot about one's personality. Whether this is true or not, studies have shown that people make judgements as shown in the table below:

| Physical facial features | Personality judged as |
|---|---|
| Thin lips | Conscientious, highly moral, respectable |
| Thick lips (in females) | Sexy, amorous |
| High forehead | Intelligent, highbrow, bright |
| Protruding eyes | Excitable, explosive |
| Positive curving mouth | Cheerful, easy-going, funny, well adjusted |
| Wrinkled face | Aggressive, determined, quick-tempered |
| Dark complexion/coarse skin | Hostile, boorish, sly |
| Make-up | Sexy, frivolous |
| Wearing spectacles | Intelligent, dependable, industrious |

The smile has attracted a good deal of attention. Ventriloquists smile, as do sophisticated liars – both to put others off. The expression helps the ventriloquist deceive observers, while in the case of the 'bare-faced' liar it makes others less alert to what is going on.

Impressive physical evidence has demonstrated not only that a smile is a consequence of feeling happy or well-contented, but also that putting on a smile can induce physiological change in body temperature, heart rate, skin resistance and so on. That is, adopting a smiling expression can lead to positive moods (and vice versa). It also has the added advantage that others tend to smile back.

Smiling may be natural or faked. The broad, genuine, expressive, spontaneous smile can be defined physiologically in terms of what muscles do to different parts of the face – lips, cheeks or eyes. There is also the wry, miserable smile, often lopsided, that indicates recognition of the vicissitudes of fate. The faked or false smile can be detected by various cues: it spreads across the face more slowly and seems to last longer; the eyes are not as narrowed or closed as in a real smile; the upper lip is often exaggerated in movement, while the lower lip is less mobile. The polite smile – often more like a grimace – is as much a sign of embarrassment as happiness.

The smiling or laughing face is often not very different from the howling or tearful face. Some people – women more than men – cry with joy; we talk about things as being 'frightfully jolly'. People sometimes laugh as a response to shock, or when embarrassed. Funeral wakes are often characterised by laughter. Genuine laughter increases breathing, while lowering blood pressure and heart rate. Crying, as uniquely human as laughing, may accompany laughter and may be as much a sign of joy and relief as of shock or sadness.

Like eye gaze, the facial expressions of people at interviews, in committee or while working with customers give powerful messages about their inner states, particularly if you observe how the expressions change in response to what is being said.

## Gestures

Hands, heads and feet can be used to produce a very wide range of signals, signs and other movements. Hand movements accompany speech and can be used to:

- point to people, objects, self
- show spatial relationships (in/outside; up/down)
- show spatial movements (round-and-round)
- beat time by showing rhythm or tempo
- show particular movement (punching, kicking)
- draw a visual picture (spiral slide, odd-shaped room).

The following are the most typical gestures and their meanings:

| Gesture | Meaning |
| --- | --- |
| Nod Head | Agreement |
| Shake fist | Anger |
| Rub palms | Anticipation |
| Clap | Approval |
| Raise hand | Seeking attention |
| Yawn | Boredom |
| Rub hands | Cold |
| Beckon | Come |
| Extend hand | Invite to dance/join in |
| Point | Give direction |
| Thumb down | Disapproval |
| Shrug shoulders | Lack of interest |
| Pat on back | Encouragement or commiseration |
| Pretend to shoot oneself | *Faux pas* |
| Outline female body | Attractive female |
| Rub stomach | Hungry |
| Wave hand | Goodbye |
| Shake hands | Greetings |

The Anglo-Saxon world is surprisingly gesture-poor, possibly because of the richness of the English language. The 'teeth flick' (meaning anger), the 'cheek screw' (meaning 'good') or the 'eyelid-pull' (meaning 'I am alert') are unknown in Britain.

It is possible to distinguish between many different types of gestures. Ekman and Friesen (1972) have distinguished between:

- *emblems*: sign language, often rude, sometimes part of a task- or occupation-specific culture. They are a shorthand (pun intended!) substitute for words.

- *illustrators*: movements that accompany and amplify speech. The size of the fish that got away and the place of the pain in the body are both illustrators.

- *regulators*: gesture movements like those of an orchestral conductor. They attempt to regulate conversation: to 'shut someone up', bring others in, encourage them to continue.

- *adaptors*: anxiety-displacement movements that may reveal emotions.

- *displays*: often ritual gestures of powerful emotions or symbolic quality, such as the clenched fist, the Nazi salute, the laying on of hands.

If a person taps his or her temple with a forefinger it can mean 'crazy' or intelligent: opposite meanings from the identical gesture. This hand-to-brain contact could mean a 'bad brain' (stupid fool) or a 'good brain' (very bright, clever). The context and the culture determine the meaning of gestures. Yet many gestures extend well beyond specific or national boundaries.

Gestures can say something of the emotional state of others, particularly their level of excitement or anxiety. Self-touching gestures are often particularly telling of shame, doubt and presentational anxieties. Gestures also give information about personality. Extroverts tend to be more expansive, while people with depression have fewer, slower, more hesitant and non-emphatic gestures. Neurotics touch their faces and hair often, scratching and pulling; they indulge in wringing and interlocking of their hands and opening and closing of their fists.

There are many gestures which in Anglo-Saxon culture are easily interpreted. These include rubbing hands together (excited expectation, or simply being cold). Clenching hands (in front of the face, on a desk or in front of the crotch) may signal confidence or frustration; steepling hands (up or down) is usually a positive gesture of confidence; thumb displays (holding your jacket lapels, sticking your thumbs out of a pocket) are thought to show superiority, even pomposity – possibly even ridicule.

Hand-to-face gestures are particularly intriguing and nicely characterised in the three monkey states called 'Hear no evil, see no evil, speak no evil'. The mouth guard, possibly disguised as a fake cough or used to conceal a yawn, is often associated with lying – as is the nose touch. It has been suggested that if a speaker touches his or her mouth he or she may be lying, while if the listener does it, it suggests that he or she feels the speaker is lying!

The eye-rub (see no evil), the ear-rub (hear no evil), and the neck-scratch, collar-tug or fingers in mouth (no nail-biting) are often seen as signs of deceit or uncertainty – or simply anxiety. It may be that anxiety or anxiety about lying causes physical tension, which leads to the gesture – rather than it being the manifestation of an unconscious idea.

Touching the chin, cheek or jaw is usually associated with thinking (evaluating what is being said or making a decision) and occasionally with boredom. Rubbing the back of the neck is often interpreted as a sign of frustration ('pain in the neck'). Folded arms or using bags, flowers or books as a barrier is usually interpreted as defensiveness or nervousness. Equally, leg or foot crossing with ankle locks is usually interpreted as coldness or defensiveness. Precisely when these gestures are adopted or changed (particularly in terms of what is being said at the same time) is a very important clue to their interpretation.

Pease (1990) has noted various other sorts of known gestures and offered interpretations:

- straddling a chair (sitting backwards) – using the back of the chair as a defence because of aggression

- fluff-picking (picking imaginary fluff off clothes) – approval or deliberately withholding evidence

- both hands behind the head – controlled, dominant, confident

-  hands on hip/in belt – sexual aggressiveness or sizing one another up

- tie-straightening – preening in males as a courtship gesture.

Equally, one can use various props like cigars, pipes and spectacles to send gestures. How and where smoke is blown, how cigarettes are held, when glasses are put in the mouth are all interpreted as meaning something whether the 'actor' meant it or not. Indeed film actors deliberately use certain actions to convey the motives and mood of their character. Anything put in the mouth may be thought of as a gesture of reassurance or possible aggression.

## Orientation

One of the few things business people can control fairly easily is the way in which one orients oneself to others. This is usually done by the way furniture is arranged. Thus one can interview across a desk (face-to-face, diametrically opposite); over the corner of a desk (at 90° in a cosy corner) or side by side facing outwards.

Orientation of the body (the pointing of torso, feet) has been thought of as indicating where people's thoughts are or where they really want to go. People standing talking can face each other at various angles (head-on, side-by-side), and they can, through orientation, include or exclude others. Opening to a triangular position indicates acceptance. Body-pointing as

Chartered Institute of Personnel and Development

# Customer Satisfaction Survey

*We would be grateful if you could spend a few minutes answering these questions and return the postcard to CIPD. <u>Please use a black pen to answer.</u> **If you would like to receive a free CIPD pen, please include your name and address.*** IPD MEMBER Y/N

......................................................................................................................................

1. Title of book .....................................................................................................................

2. Date of purchase:  month ................   year ...................

3. How did you acquire this book?
☐Bookshop   ☐Mail order   ☐Exhibition   ☐Gift   ☐Bought from Author

4. If ordered by mail, how long did it take to arrive:
☐1 week   ☐2 weeks   ☐more than 2 weeks

5. Name of shop ............................. Town...................................... Country ...........

6. Please grade the following according to their influence on your purchasing decision with 1 as least influential: (please tick)

|  | 1 | 2 | 3 | 4 | 5 |
|---|---|---|---|---|---|
| Title |  |  |  |  |  |
| Publisher |  |  |  |  |  |
| Author |  |  |  |  |  |
| Price |  |  |  |  |  |
| Subject |  |  |  |  |  |
| Cover |  |  |  |  |  |

7. On a scale of 1 to 5 (with 1 as poor & 5 as excellent) please give your impressions of the book in terms of: (please tick)

|  | 1 | 2 | 3 | 4 | 5 |
|---|---|---|---|---|---|
| Cover design |  |  |  |  |  |
| Paper/print quality |  |  |  |  |  |
| Good value for money |  |  |  |  |  |
| General level of service |  |  |  |  |  |

8. Did you find the book:
Covers the subject in sufficient depth   ☐Yes   ☐No
Useful for your work   ☐Yes   ☐No

9. Are you using this book to help:
☐In your work  ☐Personal study   ☐Both   ☐Other (please state)

*Please complete if you are using this as part of a course*

10. Name of academic institution................................................................................

11. Name of course you are following? ....................................................................

12. Did you find this book relevant to the syllabus? ☐Yes ☐No ☐Don't know

**Thank you!**

To receive regular information about CIPD books and resources call 020 8263 3387.

1795/05/00

**Publishing Department**

**Chartered Institute of Personnel and Development**

**CIPD House**

**Camp Road**

**Wimbledon**

**London**

**SW19 4BR**

well as the less obvious but also less conscious feet-pointing often indicates the person to whom ideas are addressed, who is favoured in a conversation and who is liked or disliked. Seated body orientation (as well as distance) is equally very indicative of the nature of a relationship. Chairs can be arranged to symbolise or control a relationship or may be moved over time to redefine it.

Inevitably sitting opposite a person often symbolises opposition. It is no accident the British have a two-party oppositional system given the architecture of the House of Commons. People leave restaurants more quickly when sat opposite one another, unless tables are particularly wide. Sitting side-by-side often symbolises co-operation and support but it can be uncomfortable if people are seated too close together or if they feel they are not getting enough eye-contact.

Round tables are democratic and connote co-operation. There is an organisation called the Round Table, and King Arthur's knights sat at one legendary round table. Various United Nations tables are round(ish) – symbolically indicating the equality of all in the circle. Theatre 'in the round' too has a quite different feel for both audience and actors. Round tables are becoming more popular in business. They have tended to replace the more common formal square table. Square tables can be awkward – at least some people sit diametrically opposite one another. Square tables have a more closed and exclusive feel than round tables, which appear easier to join.

Rectangular and oval tables are still found in board rooms and cabinet meetings. The person who has greatest power tends to sit in the middle or more commonly at the head, while the rank of those attending is defined in terms of distance from this person.

Most work is undertaken sitting down. Some managers have learnt the benefits of having meetings standing up. This usually ensures shorter meetings. It is considered disrespectful to lean on something (like the person at the bar, the farmer at the gate) because it signals inattention and relaxation. People still sit for most meetings. Angle and distance of chairs from one another is important but so is height. Sometimes chairs, like thrones, are elevated to symbolise power and influence.

Pease (1990) has noted that desk seating positions (at rectangular tables) can be in the:

- *corner position*: indicating friendly casual communication but with a part barrier (favoured by GPs)

- *co-operative position*: next to each other

- *co-operative defensive position*: opposite each other with the barrier between, but an understanding that half the space on the table/desk is one person's territory while the other half belongs to the other person

- *independent position*: diagonally opposite, at maximum distance, avoiding eye contact.

## Posture

A person's posture may result from early psychological rather than physical experience. Adolescents may hunch or stoop to disguise breast development or excessive height. Long periods of depression may lead to the adoption of the depressive's characteristic sagging pose even after recovery has been made. Some argue that just as body posture is an index of emotional health (tensed muscles lead to bad posture) so you can change (relax) emotional states by changing posture. Indeed the Alexander technique is based on diagnosing and correcting posture. Yoga and Chinese T'ai Ch'i aim to improve general well-being through exercising or manipulating the body.

The three main human postures are standing, sitting (which includes squatting and kneeling) and lying. Shown 'stickmen' figures, people can easily, accurately and reliably identify states of mind or qualities such as suspicion, shyness, indifference, puzzlement and so on. Thus one can signal relaxation by asymmetrical arm and leg positions, a backwards and possibly sideways lean and hand relaxation. The arms, legs and trunk alone and together can give strong messages of states such as anxiety, sexual flirtatiousness and humility.

Some researchers have noticed how body movement communicates various desires in courtship or psychotherapy. Non-verbal cues of courtship/readiness include preening the hair and adjusting the stockings. Cues from positioning include facing one another with the torso leaning inward so as to exclude others. Actions of appeal might involve flirtatious glances, crossing the legs or exposing the palm of the hand. Posture in a selection or appraisal interview can give a good indication how tense or relaxed a person is. A conference speaker's posture can also give an insight into his or her confidence.

## Touch (or body contact)

We live in a non-contact culture – hence the power of touch. Children explore the world by touch, until the inhibitions of our society penalise it. Touch has a primitive significance of heightened intimacy. In the 1960s psychotherapists used so-called 'encounter groups' and 'T-groups' to explore the therapeutic benefits of touch (among other things). Argyle (1975) noted that in Western society there are many types of body contact:

| | |
|---|---|
| *Patting* head, back | *Holding* hand, arm, knee |
| *Slapping* face, hand, bottom | *Guiding* hand, arm |
| *Punching* face, chest | *Embracing* shoulder, body |
| *Pinching* cheek, bottom | *Linking* arms |
| *Stroking* hair, face, upper body, knee | *Laying on* hands |
| *Shaking* hands | *Kicking* bottom |

*Kissing* mouth, cheek, breasts, hand, foot

*Grooming* hair, face

*Licking* face

*Tickling* anywhere

People, in Anglo-Saxon culture, touch for various reasons: in attempting to persuade or obtain a favour; when sympathising; when giving orders and advice; when excited or happy. Most people can distinguish between the professional touch (of doctors, hairdressers or aroma-therapists), the social touch (of greeting or farewell), the friendly touch (of sports people when they celebrate or families) and the sexual touch (to bring about or increase arousal).

Body contact is dictated by relationship. Touching one's spouse, children, friends, relations and strangers is governed by very different rules. Touch can signal sexual arousal, nurturance or dependence, affiliation and aggression. It is often used as an interaction signal in greetings and farewells and in guiding others. Touch is used with great meaning at grand ceremonies, such as confirmations, ordinations and weddings. It often signals the passing on of a continuous chain of authority. It is used in prize giving and initiation rites.

The handshake is one of the most over-interpreted of body signals. We are told that it is an integral part of personality and a symbol of power struggle. Whose hand is 'on top', how vice-like the grip and the weight-on-the-foot relative to the hand are all supposed to provide information. The hand has 'palm power': one can have a submissive, recipient, open gesture – like a beggar – or a more aggressive, palm-down gesture.

The handshake can be described by the nature of the grip, the power of that grip, the number of 'pumps' and who reaches first. The dominant handshake is characterised by a palm down, firm but short shake. Various typical handshakes have been described:

- *glove or politician*: both hands used by one party to cover the opponent's hand, trying to give the impression of honesty

- *dead fish*: cold, clammy, limp

- *knuckle grinder*: the macho handshake which squeezes the fingers only

- *stiff-arm thrust*: no bending of the arm

- *arm pull*: sometimes found in children.

Another interesting quandary in the 'modern' handshake is what to do with the other (left) hand. One can leave it limp at one's side, grab the other person's wrist, elbow, upper arm or shoulder to show various attitudes such as sincerity, honesty or a caring quality.

Some handshakes, of course, have no hidden meaning. Those with arthritis or those whose hands are integral to their career such as surgeons or musicians may avoid handshakes or give weak shakes, not because of their lack of confidence or power but because of their fear of damaging their hands. Handshake gestures may have been learnt in childhood and have little to do with carefully thought out patterns of dominance and submission.

## Other signals

A number of other signals are important but less well researched. Three shall be considered briefly: dress, odour and territories. Each has clear analogies in the animal world. Many animals – for example, peacocks – send signals using special feathers and markings; nearly all animals send powerful scent markers; and most have a clear defensible territory.

### Dress

The whole fashion business is designed to enable people to send signals about wealth, taste and values, as well as in- and out-group statements. Clothes make a strong visual statement about how you see yourself. They are the value system of the individual made visible. Notice the way jewellery, watches, spectacles and so on are marketed, often emphasising the communication functions of each item. Various consultants make a good living advising business people about which colours they should choose or avoid, as well as about types of material and clothes that will make them look taller, thinner, more serious or part of a particular group.

Badges, rings or cuff-links can indicate allegiance to groups or to organisations – often educational – that one has been associated with in the past. Ties, for men, can signal hobbies (golf-club designs), humour (male chauvinist pigs), as well as club membership. Spectacles can be used to emphasise facial features or to give an impression of studiousness, frivolity or practicality. The material used in attire – crocodile-skin products, ivory or fur – can indicate ecological values, or lack of them. Fashion consciousness – the keen sense of what is currently in (and out) – is another signal that may be sent by clothes. 'Power dressing' seeks to imbue the wearer with significance. People tend to accentuate and hide certain features in order to attract or distract. The signalling system of clothes is not perfect. Noise in the system originating from sub-group and cultural differences in meaning, inevitably leads to some messages becoming lost or mixed up.

Sexuality, power and wealth may be signalled by subtle dress-code cues, but only those 'in the know' can pick them up. Ultimately, dress signals personality and values more than other specific messages. One can make 'fashion statements' but only the fashion conscious can read them. There is also the rather sad spectacle of the 'fashion victim' who invests, in every sense, far too much in the signalling system. One can be taught the language of dress but it is too crude a communication system to be particularly useful.

Some people are more 'clothing aware' than others. It has

been suggested that clothing choice and awareness relate to:

- *mental health*: disturbed people wear bizarre clothing or pay little heed to their appearance

- *manipulation*: people can wear outfits aimed at deception for their own ends

- *social class*: better-educated people from a higher social class are sometimes more clothes-sensitive, though some 'at the top' flout clothes sense while some 'at the bottom' are extremely clothes-sensitive

- *self-concept*: clothes are a second skin and reveal confidence

- *social values*: clothes can indicate conservatism or radicalism, and where one stands on the practical/impractical (sensible/creative) dimension.

Uniformed organisations – such as hotels, airlines or nursing services – have to consider how their uniforms suggest not only cleanliness and efficiency but status and rank. Clients prefer to see their professionals dressed in a certain way to indicate the latters' education and know-how and to signal an appropriate relationship between 'them' and 'us'. Patients in a hospital like doctors to be smartly dressed and wearing a white coat. But clothing choice at work may be severely limited by dress codes – even by 'dress-down' days on which people are constrained to wear 'casual' clothes. Dress 'off duty' may be more revealing because it is less constrained.

Clothing has an effect on both wearer and observer. People may use clothes to try to induce a state of well-being in others. It has been demonstrated that you are more likely to give money (eg charitable donations, restaurant tips) or information to someone if you like the way he or she is dressed. The fact that clothes affect the wearer is embodied in the simple phrase 'When I look good, I feel good.'

## Odour

For too long, psychologists neglected the role of smell in communication. Odour is a powerful communication system among animals and we humans are all personally aware of the olfactory consequences of such things as stress and sexual excitement on our own bodies. People know that some smells are able to summon powerful memories. There is now considerable interest in 'pheromones', a term coined in 1959 from Greek *phero* 'to carry' and *hormao* 'to impel'. The chemical secretions are used by all primates to mark territory, assert dominance, repel rivals and attract mates.

Adults have scent glands under their arms and around their genitals; body hair traps scents which are powerful markers. It is the way in which clothes capture, turn stale and 'chemicalise' these body odours that makes them unpleasant.

People in Western societies seem determined to eradicate and replace natural body odours. For many the morning begins with the use of soap, toothpaste, mouthwash, scented shampoo, deodorant and cologne or perfume. Individuals have distinct, reliably detectable body odours (sweet, musky, lemony) that are a function of health and diet. Doctors have been urged to use their sense of smell in diagnosis.

Anthropologists have pointed out that odour communicates racial, cultural and family traits that help identify us and that relate to a range of acceptable and avoidant behaviours. Because smells are so clearly associative, environments are deliberately 'sprayed'. The smell of baking bread and freshly brewed coffee has been used to help sell houses. Some shops use the pine and spice smells of Christmas to try to induce greater sales in the festive season. Hospitals and dentists try to hide or mask smells associated with those places because of the extent to which they are associated with pain and anxiety.

To demonstrate the power of odour, one study required men on a selection skills course to evaluate the merits of a particular woman. The only difference between her and the other interviewees lay in the perfume she was wearing. Surprisingly, she was evaluated as more able and technically skilled when wearing a popular perfume. In this sense the scent gave her a 'halo effect' – smells nice, is nice; smells good, is good.

It seems that the human odour-communication system is primitive, and operates for most of us beneath the level of awareness. Few people are able to send or detect complex messages or signals by the choice of chemicals to spray on themselves, and most are not in a position voluntarily to alter the central nervous system in order to induce particular scents. Most of us operate on the pleasant/unpleasant dimension and are utterly reliant on the erratic feedback of others to determine reaction. Equally, the social problem of telling somebody about 'bad breath' or 'unpleasant odour' is fraught with embarrassment. All this leads to the conclusion that most of us have very little idea of the effect our natural and unnatural scent has on others we meet.

## Territory

The study of space is called proxemics and the study of how humans communicate through their use of time is called chronemics. Strictly speaking, territory is not a bodily signal. But we do signal differently when in different territories and we often send clear defensive messages as to what delineates a territory. Like animals, people try to establish and maintain territories, albeit fleetingly. The 'unmanned' towel on the beach, the coat on the chair and the suitcase on the seat all indicate that somebody has staked out that territory. We all know the different feel a meeting has if: it is held in the boss's office; if the boss visits you in your office; or if you meet in an assigned meeting room. Most houses have public and private rooms – areas designated appropriate for outsiders and insiders. The same is true of public buildings, eg hotels which have 'staff only' signs. Often there is a dramatic difference in the quality of decor between different territories.

Just as actors differentiate between front-of-house and back-stage, so businesses differentiate between front-house and back-room. Dress, language, posture and physical contact are all quite different in these different zones. It is possible to make distinctions between different 'psychological' zones. First, there is a very private zone in the office. It may be the employee's small but very personal workstation and locker. Then there is the shared inner-group zone of the working department or division. Here people have marked out favourite chairs and so on that are known to, and respected by, all those in the group. Comfort with interpersonal distance is a function of: sex (men have narrower intimate zones than women; culture (Anglo-Saxons like more distance than Latins); and area population density (rural people stand further away from each other than urban dwellers).

It has become common to distinguish between four zones: intimate (less than three feet), where professionals are not allowed to intrude – except medical and quasi-medical people; personal (three – four feet), which one may have to share in aeroplanes, for example; a social zone (four – 12 feet), for most strangers and colleagues at work; and a public zone.

Meetings held in public spaces are quite different from those in private space. The use of space is also very culturally different. The Japanese see the shape and arrangement of space as having clear tangible meaning. Yet in public they cling close together in crowded groups. Americans carry a two-foot bubble of privacy around themselves. For privacy, some people – for example, Arabs – retreat into themselves; others retreat behind closed doors.

Territory is important in business particularly when entering another's territory. How close one approaches the desk or chair of another is associated with status. People who enter a room and remain near the door signal lower status than those who walk right up to the executive's desk. The time between door-knocking/entering and hearing/answering is status-related. The quicker the visitor enters the room, the more status he or she has, while the longer the executive takes to answer, the more status he or she has. The senior manager can walk into a subordinate's office unannounced yet the latter has to wait outside the former's office to be let in. Subordinates leave the senior's office when the telephone rings, while the former does not always answer the phone so as to give the boss the full attention he or she deserves.

Physical areas have special significance because they are the territory of a particular person and are associated with high/low status people in particular social roles. The physical layout can determine how people use space in waiting rooms or common rooms – as designers of airports or hotels know so well. The 'trick' is to give people an experience of private territory while ensuring the maximum number of people use the facility.

Body language is made up of the various signals detailed

above: the quick glance, the wry smile, the well-known gesture, body posture, the light touch, the badge on the lapel and the choice of perfume. Each, alone and together, can provide a powerful and subtle form of communication to complement the spoken language.

# 3 body language and business

## The business of communication

A great deal of any manager's business is about communication. Managers have to persuade and delegate, negotiate and motivate, buy and sell. They have to do presentations to the board, chair small committee meetings and counsel individuals.

But business is about more than skilfully and sensitively putting across one's message. It is also about reading the signals from others. Negotiators, like poker players, have to try to distinguish bluff, bravado and bravura from the actual position the 'opponents' are in. Small nuances and subtle changes over time are eagerly scanned for evidence of a change in position. Understanding how an employee is reacting to a negative appraisal can be greatly helped by body language. And, of course, watching for signals in a potential buyer is an important part of the successful salesperson's job.

Equally importantly, organisations realise that the physical environment can have an important impact on the communication patterns – and ultimately the productivity – of employees. Being seated at a square, oval or a round table inevitably affects eye-contact patterns. Having meetings standing up gives clues about posture. Where meetings are held – that is, on whose territory – can make participants feel less or more confident. Communicating by letter or e-mail has different consequences from making telephone calls, and these are different again from those of face-to-face teleconferencing.

The practical application of a thorough 'scientific' knowledge of body communication is supposedly that various techniques can be learnt to read others' secret thoughts and motives, and hence to have some control over them. Some people believe that salespeople are trained in these techniques so as somehow to manipulate a possible customer into buying a product against his or her better judgement. This is simply not true. Salespeople are taught various techniques, but these are aimed more at relaxing the customers and understanding their anxieties.

## Body language and selling

Consider the car showroom and what salesmen have been trained to do. Most showrooms have three different areas: the reception desk, the car display area and the relaxation (sofa) area. The customer meets the salesperson behind the desk. This is a formal area where particulars may be obtained. Soon, however, customers are encouraged to inspect the vehicle. Salespeople encourage the customer to sit in the driving seat. But they leave the door open, go around to the other side of the car and crouch at the same height talking through the open door. Thus both front doors are open. Experience has shown that customers, especially women, can take fright if the door is closed. It has also shown that talking to people from a similar height position makes people more collaborative and questioning.

Salespeople rarely show customers the engine by opening the bonnet because it serves mainly to frighten and confuse, and to remind them of what can go wrong. Salespeople are trained to watch eye movements carefully to see what customers are 'really' interested in – boot space, baby seats, wheel trims. Customers are encouraged to touch and later drive the car: to mark it as theirs.

The third phase often takes place in the lounge area, where sofas are arranged in a semi-circle or at right angles. It is here that other discussions occur, covering residual questions the customer may have. The final signing, however, takes place at the desk.

Salespeople know not to touch the customers but they encourage them to touch the product. They know the importance of the 'new car smell' and of interpreting the customers' movements and glances. They have to know when 'no' means 'yes' and vice versa; when one customer needs to be sold the product on its technical specifications and another on its family-friendliness.

## Emotional intelligence and reading the signals

For the last 15 years the idea that EQ or Emotional Intelligence Quotient is more important in business than IQ or Intelligent Quotient has been taking hold. EQ is defined as inter- and intrapersonal intelligence. It has been argued that it consists of three categories of adaptive abilities, all of which are related to sending and reading non-verbal signals. They are the expression of emotion, the regulation of emotion in oneself and others, and the utilisation of emotion in solving problems. Different writers on the topic have emphasised slightly different things but all stress the importance of (i) the perception, appraisal and expression of emotion; and (ii) understanding, analysing and emphasising emotional knowledge.

In short, EQ is about emotional literacy, and emotional literacy is about reading the cues of non-verbal communication. But it should be pointed out that it includes the ability to send, receive *and* regulate cues. Many neurotics are very sensitive to the moods and feelings of others. Often they can partly disguise their own feelings – but not usually for long, as they find it difficult to regulate their own moods. The high-EQ person is more resilient and psychologically robust than most neurotics. He or she knows how to find and sustain positive emotions and tends to be optimistic, with a strong ego.

But high-EQ people know when to speak or indeed listen to others about personal problems, when to share emotions with others, how to present a good impression of themselves and how to complement and charm others. In the chapter 'Managing with Heart' in his book *Emotional Intelligence* (Bloomsbury, 1996) Goleman argued that teamwork, open lines of communication, co-operation, listening and speaking one's mind are characteristics of emotional intelligence (EI) and are essential at work.

In business, empathy and compassion are in, and the manipulative jungle-fighter boss out. Leadership and being a good manager is about being attuned to the feelings of those people managers have to deal with (up, sideways and down). There are three basic applications of EI – being able to see grievances as helpful critiques, which is using feedback effectively; creating an atmosphere in which diversity is valued rather than a source of friction; and networking effectively.

But would you prefer the CEO of your company to have a high EQ or a high IQ? Do you want a cold but clever boss, who understands the business, keeps his or her eye firmly on the bottom line, reads the market signals, but is a little clumsy, shy and gauche? Or would you prefer the perceptive, empathic, socially adept boss, equally able to charm customers, employees and the media? Naturally it is desirable to have both, but what are the consequences of being all head with no heart, or vice versa?

The former, high-IQ person may be respected but not particularly liked, whereas the latter is often greatly loved but not respected for his or her business acumen. It is not usual to find a boss with both high IQ and high EQ. Perhaps the best solution is to have a good mix of IQ and EQ on the board – but could they get on with each other? One does suspect that the bright board members might despise the warm, sensitive ones, who in turn might be offended by what they would perceive as intellectual arrogance.

But the good news is that whereas IQ cannot be learnt, EQ can. You can learn various intellectual tricks, but it really is not likely that you can raise your (adult) IQ much. On the other hand, it is relatively easy to acquire EQ skills through 'social skills', 'interpersonal skills', 'assertiveness', 'counselling' and 'communication skills' courses.

## The medium for the message

Some people in business prefer to communicate certain messages in writing while others prefer using face-to-face meetings. Research has shown that the choice of a communication medium can greatly affect the degree of clarity or ambiguity of the message being sent. Oral media (for example, telephone conversations and face-to-face meetings) are preferable to written media such as notes and memos when messages are ambiguous (requiring a great deal of assistance in interpreting them), whereas written media are preferable when messages are clear.

What leads someone to choose one mode or medium of communication rather than another? Why drop a note in a pigeon-hole as opposed to phoning? Why race up three floors to find a person not in when you could have used an e-mail?

One obvious answer to the question of choice of medium is economy and efficiency. Telephones are faster, letters and memos can be duplicated – and so on. However, there are various important psychological advantages and disadvantages to the various media that are well understood but seldom explicitly discussed. Certain face-to-face or video-conferenced communication offers the best option for sending and receiving body language cues.

## Verbal communication media

Consider the letter or its electronic equivalent – the e-mail. It has a number of obvious advantages. Unlike the telephone call or face-to-face meeting (unless this is audio- or video-taped), the letter or printed e-mail is a record of communication. Hence, it is the preferred medium of lawyers, bureaucrats and others concerned with the extraction of money or information. The letter, particularly if produced on the ubiquitous word-processor, may also be revised so that a precise tone, meaning or ambiguity may be communicated. Letters and e-mails are a more private means of communication than the telephone or face-to-face meeting, and in some instances they are cheaper than other methods. However, there are some doubts about the security of e-mails.

Curiously, however, two of the major drawbacks of the letter are also its major advantages. Letters take time and feedback is postponed. We tend to impart bad news in writing when we feel inadequate about dealing with the feedback we might receive. Angry but unassertive people of all ages frequently write letters and e-mails of complaint after receiving poor service, rather than dealing with the matter immediately – often because they are afraid of the negative, aggressive or direct feedback they are likely to receive.

We also write when the feedback is likely to embarrass us. People who have recently become bereaved, and sometimes the dying themselves, often explain how they received many letters, gifts and flowers but, strangely, people infrequently visited. As people usually respond in the same medium through which they were initially contacted, the caring friend can expect nothing more threatening than a grateful acknowledgement letter.

Another advantage of the letter – but less so of the e-mail – is the opportunity it offers for impression-management. First there are the letter-heading and logo features, as well as the quality of the paper. Some people immediately rub the letter heading like a Braille reader just to check it is embossed. Business letter-headed notepaper is used to identify with the organisation. Letters also allow one to state formally one's qualifications and job title.

## Vocal communication media

The telephone offers numerous advantages over the letter. Feedback is immediate, if you catch the person in. It has a rather different legal status – that is there is no record. One can queue jump often quite effectively, unless the person with whom one wishes to speak has a filter mechanism such as an unhelpful PA.

But the telephone has two other major advantages certainly over the face-to-face meeting. The first is that you may speak to somebody while knowing practically nothing about him or her. What psychological or demographic variables can one recognise from a telephone voice? Sex? Probably, although we have no doubt all made embarrassing mistakes in this area. Age? Perhaps people under 10 or over 80 years sound different but it is very difficult to make accurate judgements. Education, race? Very unlikely. What about detecting a person's emotions or whether he or she is lying? Again, unless at the extremes of anger, fear or depression, it is very difficult to detect a person's mood or indeed his or her implicit intentions when communicating over the telephone. We have all, no doubt, experienced surprise at seeing a favourite radio personality on television and finding that he or she is older or younger, balder or more hirsute, plainer or more attractive than one has imagined. Indeed, radio presenters' looks and shape may account precisely for why they are on radio as opposed to television in the first place.

Of course, not knowing much about the other person may be advantageous to either party. Just as you cannot know the age, looks or handicaps of the person to whom you are talking on the telephone, neither can he or she know much about you. Hence the use of a 'telephone voice' – an attempt to present an image through accent and tone of voice that is specious but desirable. The telephone offers some of the major advantages of face-to-face communication, such as speed of feedback, but crucially hides none of the tell-tale non-verbal cues which allow one to detect how honest, sincere, committed, truthful and so on is the person with whom we are talking.

The telephone offers one other major advantage – although there may be exceptions to the rule. Because one pays for a call in terms of a multiple of time and distance, the average time spent on the telephone is probably considerably shorter than the average time spent face-to-face discussing exactly the same problem. Niceties and trivia are usually reduced and one gets down to the point of the communication far more quickly. People may feel the need to provide refreshments when meeting face-to-face, or may be interrupted by a third party. With the exception of those made by adolescent females, however, telephone calls are fortunately rarely too long and furthermore one has a whole host of possible excuses (lies) why they should be terminated (kettle boiling, knock at the door and so on).

But most people prefer to communicate face-to-face although of course in doing so they lose some of the advantages of the letter and the telephone outlined above. They need more than verbal (written) and vocal (audio) cues to give and receive complex messages. Academic ethnologists, zoologists and psychologists have tended to rewrite the songwriter's words – 'It's not what you say, it's the way that you say it' – so emphasising the role of non-verbal cues, such as eye-gaze patterns, body posture, movements, gestures and the like in communication. The crucial point is the medium you choose to 'say it' through.

### Remembering what you read and see

Imagine the following scenario. A large group of people with very similar backgrounds is randomly divided into three smaller groups. One group watches a 15-minute television programme (say a news broadcast); another listens to the identical programme, but without the benefit of pictures; a third has 15 minutes to read the news broadcaster's script. They all get the same information: the television group gets visual, vocal and verbal (audio-visual) data; the radio group gets vocal and verbal (audio-only) data; and the print group gets verbal (script-only) data. Shortly after the exposure, members of each group are asked questions testing their free recall of all they can remember, and their recall of answers to specific questions. Which group remembers the most and is most accurate? In short, who shows better recall? Many studies have shown, to people's surprise, that the print group (those who read) remembered most, and the television group (those who watched) remembered least. Put another way, having additional body-language information leads, paradoxically, to poorer memory. We are constantly told of the 'power of television' and yet studies are fairly consistent on the point that we remember least of what we see, more of what we read. What is the explanation for this somewhat paradoxical finding?

## Depth of processing

Reading requires more mental effort, more processing of material. Reading the words and when appropriate conjuring up mental images involves more concentration, which can and does result in better memory. Looking at the television is associated with relaxation rather than learning, even when we are told to concentrate.

## Speed of reading

Although radio and television presenters are taught to read at a particular pace and in a style that is maximally intelligible, not all people prefer the pace. When reading one's own material, one can go at one's own pace. Difficult material, unfamiliar jargon, reading in a second language all demand a slower pace to make the text comprehensible.

## Visual interference

Except in advertisements, it is often the case that the pictures and the storyline are not perfectly synchronised. This is often the case with the news, but occurs very frequently in television as a whole. Particularly when the pictures involve violence or emotional anxiety people pay little attention to the story line! Thus while they may remember a great deal about the news reader's colour of tie, or the images of people tending graves, they do not recall salient features of the story.

### Paragraphing and textual chunking

Newspaper and magazine editors are rightly very concerned with layout because they know this helps to present information in easily comprehensible bites. The chunking of stories is more difficult on radio and television.

The lesson to be learnt is this: when meeting people face-to-face we are privileged to obtain verbal (what they say), vocal (how they say it) and visual cues (what they look like). But paying close attention to foot-tapping or changes in the pace or tone of voice can mean that we pay less attention to equally interesting and important material – what is being said. Magicians know the importance of distracting attention. Being over sensitive to non-verbal behaviour also has its costs – not remembering very well what was said.

# 4 communicating attitudes, emotions and personality

## Showing emotions

Body language sends messages. It sends messages about emotions, attitudes and personality. Therapists have argued that it can shed new light on the dynamics of inter-family relationships: that, at times, it is a signal from the unconscious. This is because, to a large extent, we express our emotions most clearly through body language. We do this partly because we cannot help it; we can 'do no other' because strong states like guilt, shame, embarrassment, anger, boredom and sexual excitement have strong physiological reactions. We 'leak' our emotions because our central nervous system reactions can cause blushing, sweating, pupil dilations, changes in breathing and so on.

We also express our emotions non-verbally because we do not always have the vocabulary to express them verbally. Occasionally, people do not have enough insight into their emotions or needs to report them – even if they wanted to do so. Indeed it has been reported that on occasion people notice their physiological reactions and non-verbal communication and infer their emotional state from them. Thus if I notice I am sweating, I conclude that I am anxious.

Various body signals are related to the messages we send. Facial expressions, eye movements, gestures, posture and tone of voice all deliberately (or not) give clear impressions about how we feel. As part of growing up in our culture we learn how to decode emotions in other people. There are tests that allow researchers to investigate the accuracy and reliability with which people will interpret a combination of signals such as anger, contempt, disgust, fear, joy or surprise.

*Messages of body language*

| NVC | Accompaniments of speech | Attitudes | Emotions | Personality and role | Ritual |
|---|---|---|---|---|---|
| Appearance | | X | | X | X |
| Head-nods | X | | | | |
| Facial expression | X | X | X | X | |
| Gaze | X | X | | X | X |
| Spatial behaviour | | X | | X | X |
| Touch | | X | X | X | X |
| Posture | | X | X | X | X |
| Gestures | X | X | X | X | X |

## Communicating attitudes

We also communicate interpersonal attitudes through body language. There are clear signals for friendliness and hostility. Watching two people talk, even without hearing the content of their speech, it is possible to understand who is – or at least feels – dominant and who is or feels submissive. For instance, liking, or affiliation, is sent as a message by:

- a higher incidence of body contact such as touching or stroking

- closer proximity in standing or sitting

- an orientation to each other which is often side-by-side

- more mutual gaze or smiling

- a posture with more leaning forward, more open arms and legs

- a softer, quieter tone of voice.

Equally, human hostility signals can look remarkably like those of animals – with harsher voices, more frowning, more teeth showing and a tense posture.

There is evidence of all sorts of sex differences but those are also related to particular personality types and particular cultures. Thus, compared to men, it seems women adopt a more open-arm, open-leg posture to males they like and those of higher status. Males, compared to females, show more evidence of vigilance in relation to physical threat – more direct orientation, more eye gaze and a much less relaxed posture. In general, people with psychotic disorders are very poor readers of body language, while neurotics are particularly good, being highly sensitive to signals of rejection. Overall, women seem more sensitive than men, particularly where the latter are in technical professions. Most often we disclose our emotions by displacement activities – behaviours designed to cope with anxiety, aggression or boredom. People waiting for an interview may go through excessive preening/grooming (brushing clothes, checking jewellery) and eating, drinking or smoking without needing to, as well as recognisable behaviours such as foot-tapping, fiddling with objects and pretend reading (flicking through magazines or newspapers without really taking anything in).

*Crowding at concerts or cinemas, in elevators and on trains or buses results in unavoidable intrusion into other people's intimate zones, and reactions to this invasion are interesting to observe. There is a list of unwritten rules that people in Western cultures follow rigidly when faced with a crowded situation such as a packed lift or public transport. These rules include the following:*

- *You are not permitted to speak to anyone, including a person you know.*

- *You must avoid eye contact with others at all times.*

- *You are to maintain a 'poker face' – no emotion must be displayed.*

- *If you have a book or newspaper, you must appear to be deeply engrossed in it.*

- *In elevators, you are compelled to watch the floor numbers above your head.*

*We often hear words like 'miserable', 'unhappy' and 'despondent' used to describe people who travel to work in the rush hour on public transport. These labels are used because of the blank, expressionless look on the faces of the travellers, but they are misjudgements on the part of the observer. What the observer sees, in fact, is a group of people adhering to the rules that apply to the unavoidable invasion of their intimate zones in a crowded public place.*

A. Pease, *Body Language: How to read others' thoughts*, 1990, p22, London, Sheldon Press.

## *Some non-verbal signs in everyday conversation*

| | | |
|---|---|---|
| *Seeking information* | **Paralanguage** | Higher duration of utterance, faster reaction-time latency, more speech interruption |
| | **Visual** | More frequent gazes in the direction of the other speaker |
| | **Proxemic** | Shorter spacial distance in standing or seating arrangements |
| *Permission to speak* | **Paralanguage** | More frequent head nods and chin thrusts, more expansive hand and feet movements, larger postural shifts |
| | **Visual** | Larger pupil size, increased eye-blinking |
| *Surprised response* | **Paralanguage** | Reduced verbalisations |
| | **Facial** | Raised brows, eyelids opened wider, dropped jaw, open mouth |
| | **Visual** | Increased pupil size, change in eye contact, raised hands |

## Intuition

To describe someone as perceptive, intuitive and insightful may refer to his or her being non-verbally literate. Some professionals have to be good at reading bodily cues so that they can understand their clients better. Psychologists and GPs, waiters and comedians, after-dinner speakers and lawyers gain a great deal if they are able to understand the motives, reactions and emotional state of their 'clients'.

A central question remains as to whether both the giving and receiving of non-verbal behaviour is innate or culturally learned and transmitted. Certainly we know through studying, for instance, the facial expressions of blind people or the touch behaviour of those from different continents, that non-verbal behaviour has biologically adaptive origins but also cultural modifications. Smiling, shaking the head for no and the shoulder-shrug are pretty universal. But others are learnt. And they are learnt as part of growing up. Witness the child, the adolescent and the adult telling a lie. As adults, most of us have learnt to be less obvious and more sophisticated in our non-verbal behaviour when we lie. This makes us, and indeed everybody else, more difficult to read. Yet it remains difficult to sustain for long either the faking or repression of emotions that have been manifested non-verbally.

Yet we all know that much non-verbal behaviour is governed by rules. Thus Debretts notes:

*One of the features of a civilised country is every person's right to privacy, even in public, and for this reason distracting behaviour of any kind – speaking loudly, shouting in the street, excessive gesticulation, whistling, singing, playing radios or arguing – breaches good manners.*

Some non-verbal behaviour is nothing more than rule-following. But what one can intuitively tell from seeing 'good manners' non-verbally is that people know the rules and are prepared to conform to them. Not following the rules could mean either ignorance of, or antagonism towards, social etiquette.

It has been suggested that women are more intuitive than men, that they are better readers of non-verbal signals and, as a consequence, more skilful senders of body cues. This may well be true. It may be a function of biological differences – the need for women in childcare to be very sensitive to the signals of their pre-verbal children. Or it may be because the structure of society means that women are often less powerful than men. Inevitably subordinates are more attentive to the moods, needs and whims of their superiors than vice versa. This interpretation may help account for women's increased sensitivity to non-verbal cues – often referred to as intuition.

## Your personality is showing

Can one understand another person's personality from his or her body language? All personality theorists are agreed that two of the absolutely fundamental dimensions of human personality are extroversion and neuroticism. Both can be reasonably accurately inferred from a close reading of body language. Extroverts tend to be active, sociable, impulsive, expressive, irresponsible risk-takers not prone to reflection. Neuroticism is characterised by low self-esteem, unhappiness, anxiety, obsessiveness, guilt and hypochondria.

### Extroversion
We all know extroverts are loud, outgoing, talkative. But few understand the 'mechanism' behind the trait. In short, extroverts are 'stimulus-hungry', under-aroused, in need of excitement.

Typical extroverts are sociable, have many friends, need to have people to talk to. They crave excitement, take chances, often stick their necks out, act on the spur of the moment, and are generally impulsive individuals. They are fond of practical jokes, always have a ready answer, and generally like changes. They are carefree, easy-going, optimistic and like to 'laugh and be merry'. They prefer to keep moving and doing things, tend to be aggressive and lose their temper quickly.

Typical introverts are quiet and retiring, introspective, fond of books rather than people. They are reserved and distant except to intimate friends. They tend to plan ahead, 'look before they leap' and distrust the impulse of the moment. They like a well-ordered mode of life and keep their feelings under close control. They seldom behave in an aggressive manner, and do not like losing their temper easily. They are

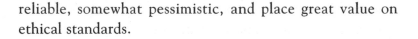

reliable, somewhat pessimistic, and place great value on ethical standards.

Extroverts trade off accuracy for speed in their search for excitement. They are more likely to have accidents, more likely to break the law, more likely to take drugs and smoke. The exhibitionistic thrill-seeking of the extroverts is as biologically hard-wired as the peace-seeking of the introverts who are quite content with a book, a chess game or a stroll in the fields. Physiologically over-aroused, the introvert is as stressed by more stimulation as the extrovert is pleased by it.

Hence the extrovert sees the introvert as boring, inadequate and secretive, whilst the introvert sees the extrovert as attention-seeking, shallow and noisy. The two extremes choose different environments in which to do differently preferred jobs with colleagues of their own type. Ambiverts, to use the correct term for those of us in the middle of the spectrum, tend to get on fairly well with both types as long as they are not too extreme.

Extreme extroverts are fairly easy to detect non-verbally. They move and talk faster than normal, tend to fidget more and are more prone to boredom. Extroverts look and touch more than introverts, prefer more dramatic clothes, gesticulate more dramatically and show a wider range of facial expressions. But it is in the area of language that introversion – extroversion can be clearly detected. Extroverts will talk faster than introverts, have fewer unfilled pauses in their speech and be quicker to respond in everyday speech.

It is suggested that extroverts differ from introverts on a number of speech and language dimensions: *form*, which refers to the degree of formality in the language used; *grammar*, which refers to the type of words that a person chooses to use; *vocabulary* or lexicon, which refers to how many words are used, and how correct and how unusual they are; *accent*, which refers to regional and class-related ways of pronouncing words and phrases; *speed*, which refers quite obviously to the speed at which people talk; and *paralanguage*, which refers to dysfluencies like 'ums', 'ers' and so on. What is being suggested in the table 'Possible speech variations according to personality traits' is that, compared to extroverts, introverts generally use more formal speech with more careful grammatical constructions, perhaps a bigger vocabulary, and so on.

*Possible speech variations according to personality traits*

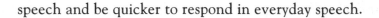

| | Traits | |
| --- | --- | --- |
| Speech and language | Introvert | Extrovert |
| Form | High | Low |
| Code | Elaborated | Restricted |
| Grammar | More nouns, adjectives, prepositions | More verbs, adverbs, pronouns |
| Vocabulary | Correct | Loose |
| Accent | Received pronunciation | Local |
| Speed | Slow | Fast |
| Paralanguage | Few dysfluencies | Many dysfluencies |

## Neuroticism

Emotionally unstable people – those with negative effectivity – are not difficult to spot. For instance, they seem to have more headaches than stable people. Of course it may be that they simply notice headaches more than stable people, or call attention to them more often. But the traits associated with neurosis are well known: being anxious, moody, lonely, pessimistic. Such people tend to have more phobias and are more prone to depression.

It is not difficult to spot clues to neurosis in a person, though it may be confusing if one person's emotional instability is primarily a function of anxiety, but in someone else one of depression. Consider the following:

- The anxious person and the depressed person seem to adopt expressions of surprise, fear and gloom that stay with them. Actors know how to present the model of a depressed person facially – the scowl, the lack of expression.

- Depressed people tend to avoid eye contact whereas anxious people dart about in the gaze pattern, ever on the outlook for potential threat. Overall the emotionally stable establish more mutual eye gaze for longer periods than the emotionally unstable.

- Depressed people show a few, hesitant, non-emphatic gestures while the anxious are more prone to self-touching, along with aimless fidgeting.

- The posture of the depressed person is easy to recognise. They look limp, lacking in energy – even ashamed.

- It is in the area of body contact that one can see emotional instability most clearly. Neurotics are often fearful of all contact. The obsessionality and hypochondria associated with neurosis makes people fearful of catching disease by touching. Neurotics with low self-esteem worry about how 'touch-worthy' they are. The guilt factor in neurosis can associate touching with sexual advances and hence it is unlikely to occur.

Certainly, by observing people over time in a range of situations one can get a pretty good idea of their personalities from their non-verbal behaviour.

## Culture and bodily communication

Since Darwin it has been acknowledged that some forms of bodily communication, like smiling and crying facial expressions, are innate, while others are learnt. When, what and why we look and how we point or stand are conditioned in childhood. There are etiquette books that tell us which particular forms of bodily communication are 'correct' or desirable. Children are constantly reminded, encouraged, rewarded and punished in the home and at school for particular kinds of bodily communication that differ from country to country.

As a consequence, there are recognised and reliable cultural differences in non-verbal communication. Consider differences in greetings: in parts of Europe it is appropriate to bow with a slight click of the heels; in Japan, the deep respectful bow is required; the gallant hand kiss is used in France; the bear-hug is popular in Russia; Thai and Indian people use a peaceful 'hands-together in prayer' gesture; the Anglo Saxons use a hand-shake. Interpersonal distance, eye gaze and bodily contact are culture-dependent, as is the taboo on exposing parts of the body, including the palm of the hand, the sole of the foot and so on. Two strong, isolated cultures such as those of the Japanese and the Arabs may have very different, indeed opposite, languages of non-verbal communication.

There are many reasons why bodily communication differs from one culture to another. It may in part be due to language usage: the number and subtlety of words for a feeling or an act must affect the necessity or preference for a non-verbal behaviour in expressing that feeling or act. The social etiquette of a people sets out precise rules about non-verbal behaviour. Books of manners set out very clearly how people are to behave. Non-verbal communication is also seen in the structure of society and in its subcultures. These lower-status groups have prescribed and proscribed ways of dealing with those from higher groups. Even differences in technology from one society to another can influence non-verbal behaviour. The use of the telephone may increase sensitivity to tones of voice.

The fact that body communication is in part culture-specific means that inter-cultural communication is fraught with potential problems. Argyle (1994) has noted that Westerners often find interacting with the Japanese difficult because they are bewildered by the Japanese people's blank facial expressions and unexpected bursts of laughter.

North Europeans find that South Europeans (and North Africans) stand too close to each other and touch too much. In one celebrated study, an observer watched how many times couples touched each other in restaurants: in Puerto Rico it was 180 times per hour, in Paris 110 times per hour and in London couples did not touch at all.

Cross-cultural body communication at work is particularly fraught with problems – hence the many books on protocol, customs and business etiquette for particular regions. The lesson is often that one country's good manners is another's grand *faux pas*. Eating and drinking, greeting and the giving of gifts are all very culture-bound and require a knowledge of correct behaviour. Gestures too do not travel: thumb joined to forefinger in a circle denotes OK in the USA, zero in France, money in Japan and is an obscene gesture in middle Europe. The depth and frequency of bowing carry meanings in Japan but nowhere else. Certainly the dos and taboos of body communication in international business can lead to misunderstanding.

# 5 lying: revealing and concealing information

## Leaking the truth

More than anything else business people hope to catch liars by carefully analysing the body language of others. Most believe that the body always betrays the mind, that the torso leaks the whole truth and that the trained and perceptive observer can 'spot the "porkie" a mile off'. If only that were true!

There are some facts that are clearly true about lying:

1   You can observe stress signals produced by the autonomic nervous system: dry mouth, sweaty palms, shallow uneven breathing, 'tickly' nose and throat, blushing or blanching. These are observable when someone is under stress whether he or she is lying or not. It is very easy to confuse the two. Most people in interviews are, initially at any rate, anxious.

2   People are less conscious of their feet or legs: the further you are from the face the nearer you get to the truth. Sudden changes in foot-tapping, pointing feet to the exit ('I want to get out of here'), simultaneous tight arm- and foot-crossing have all been taken to indicate lying. Yet active extroverts fidget more, as do young children.

Foot movements may be as reliable an index of boredom as they are of lying. The frequent crossing of legs may simply indicate an uncomfortable chair.

3    Posture is more sincere than gesture: it can be seen as more unnatural and forced when people lie. Because people seem less aware of their total posture, they may secretly signal various desires (to leave) or that they are holding back the truth. However, the shape and comfort of furniture naturally have something to do with it.

4    Give-away, expansive gestures decline: because they feel they may be caught, liars tend to sit on their hands, fold their arms, clasp their hands together. The lack of spontaneity may be an index of lying or fear – the fear of being caught. And some people are simply not as gesturally expressive as others.

5    Shifty gazes: when children are lying they look down or away. They look guilty but do not look you in the eye. Many an innocent person has been accused of lying because they avoid eye contact. But people avoid eye contact for many different reasons – they feel uncertain about their opinions, they are trying to remember facts or they feel social embarrassment. Indeed it is impolite in some cultures to look someone in the eye.

We know that people prefer, and are better at, concealment rather than falsification. It is easier to forget than to distort the truth. Falsification means 'making up' things that are not true. It is self-evidently much easier to say things did not happen at all rather than to invent a 'new story'. It is also true that people do have more problems lying about emotions – particularly powerful emotions like terror, rage, fear and despair. Recounting a story of events 50 years ago, some people cannot suppress their emotions, which manifest in their tears and trembling voice. The more ego-involving the activity, the more likely it is that people in all walks of life will have difficulty disguising the truth.

Regular and sophisticated liars have found the best mask, or cover, for their lie in the smile. Smiling has numerous advantages: it is an easy and natural expression to make voluntarily; it is polite; but, most importantly, it conceals the opposite emotion (dread, fear, anxiety).

## Different types of lie

There are different types of lie. First, there is the white, social, harmless, flattering, expedient lie: this is supposed to result from the desire to improve social intercourse by protecting another person's feelings. It is thought of as common and even beneficial – and is unlikely to cause the teller embarrassment! For many, white lies do not count as lies and are even considered a sign of social skill. Second, there is the professional, entertaining, necessary, salesman's lie: expedient lying that distorts or omits in the cause of business. For some this is good business practice – but that really depends on whether one is the buyer or the seller. Certainly a case can be made for not telling patients or subordinates how serious a situation is, as it would only make things worse.

However, not to mention the very unhappy provenance of a particular product – for example, a car that has been in a major crash – may be considered a serious lie of omission. But it is the third type of lie that is naturally of most concern to those in business – the illegal, pathological trickster's lie, the lie of omission, in which vital truths are omitted, and the lie of commission, in which facts are distorted. It is difficult to ascertain the number of these types of lie that occur in business. Suffice it to say that their consequences can be great.

## Lying in interviews

Psychologists make a number of distinctions when looking at lying in the interview. One is between *attribution* – the tendency to attribute only desirable characteristics to oneself – and *denial* – the tendency to deny undesirable characteristics. In effect, both may occur together, although people do seem to prefer one to the other. Another distinction is made between *self-deception* – when people believe their own positive self-reports or lies – and *impression management* – when respondents consciously dissimulate to create the 'right' impression.

Another crucial feature of the 'interview lie' is whether the person knows they are not telling the truth.

Some people cannot, as opposed to will not, tell the truth. Some genuinely believe they are intelligent, insightful, humorous and so on, when all the evidence suggests that they are not. In this sense they are not lying, but neither are they telling the truth. They are self-deceiving, which is different from 'putting on a good impression', and which may involve serious lies of omission or commission.

## Spotting a liar

Experts, pundits and researchers – they are not the same – often get called in by the media to help analyse whether a (famous) person is telling the truth. The Clinton – Lewinsky issue is a good example. Usually all they have to go on is brief video-clips. Yet despite this they are frequently fairly confident about their verdicts on whether a person is lying. When the experts are cross-examined on what they look for, they frequently say the following:

### *Verbal cues*

- Response latency – the time elapsing between the end of a question and the beginning of the response. Liars take longer. They hesitate more than they do when not lying.

- Linguistic distance – not saying 'I', 'he' or 'she' but talking in the abstract even when recalling incidents in which he or she was involved.

- Slow but uneven speech – the individual tries to think while speaking but gets caught out. He or she might suddenly speak fast, implying something is less significant. It is the change in pace in response to a particular question that gives a clue that something is not right.

- Over eagerness to fill silences – to keep talking when it is unnecessary. Liars overcompensate and seem uncomfortable with what are often quite short pauses.

- Too many 'pitch raises' – that is, instead of the pitch dropping at the end of a reply it raises like a question. It may sound like 'Do you believe me now?'

### Non-verbal cues

- Squirming/shifting around too much in the chair.

- Having too much – rather than too little – eye contact, as liars tend to overcompensate. They know that liars avoid mutual gaze so they 'prove they are not lying' by a lot of looking… but 'a tad too much'.

- Micro-expression or flickers of expressions – of surprise, hurt, anger. These are difficult to see unless the frames of the video are frozen.

- An increase in comfort gestures – touching his or her own face and upper body.

- An increase in stuttering, slurring and, of course, 'Freudian slips'. Generally an increase in speech errors.

- A loss of resonance in the voice – it becomes flatter, less deep, more monotonous.

For many observers the problem is in distinguishing between lying and anxiety. The well-trained and arrogant liar may thus look innocent, the truthful but nervous witness look like a liar. The fast, nervous ticks of the latter may be seen as classic signs of subordination – as if caught.

Considerable and impressive research has been carried out on lying. The research may involve videotaping people when they are known to be lying and also when they are known to be telling the truth. From an analysis of their 'normal' non-lying interpersonal style, one can see the difference when they are actually lying. And one can vary the type of lie involved to see whether this makes any difference. One can perform these studies on men as against women, professionals as against tradespeople; neurotics as against the stable and so on in order to look at individual difference patterns.

## Studying the known liar

The results of these carefully analysed studies have shown some important trends which help indicate some of the non-verbal signs of lying:

1   Decrease in the frequency of hand gestures (illustrators). People think these 'give them away' so they sit on their hands, clasp the chair and so on. This is particularly noticeable in extroverts and those who are particularly non-verbally expansive.

2   Hand-to-face contact often increases – especially nose-touching – partly because of the need to block the lie or to pull it back unconsciously into the mouth, and partly because tension in the nasal cavity can lead to tickling.

It must be noted that some people are in the habit of touching their mouth and nose more often than others, even though they are not lying. It may be to adjust their uncomfortable or poorly fitting spectacles. It may also be because they are anxious about their lipstick.

3   Increase in body shifts or squirming, saying 'I wish I were somewhere else.'

4   Increase in hand shrugs, as if disclaiming responsibility or proclaiming ignorance, whether it is relevant to the questions or not.

5   Increase in micro-expressions of the face – brief but detectable expressions of surprise, pain or doubt.

These five findings seem very robust.

### Why do some liars get caught?

Psychopaths rarely get caught lying in everyday life. Politicians, doctors and salespeople have had to learn to disguise emotions and present their case in a particular way. But other people cannot keep a 'poker face' and so get caught telling the most innocent of lies. They even tell you so. Essentially five reasons account for why liars get caught:

● lack of preparation: not ensuring that their story line is developed, consistent or verifiable; not checking certain facts. The more complex the lie, the more preparation is required.

■ lying about feelings (emotional escapes): it is easier to lie about facts than feelings; sadness, anger and so on return in the re-telling, but if they are not there this may indicate lying. It is particularly difficult to sustain a lie about a powerful emotional experience like an accident or a crime.

▲ feelings about lying: old-fashioned guilt, the more people realise or believe they are telling a serious lie, the more likely they are to show guilt. Such deception-guilt arises more from the action of lying than from the lie itself. It increases when the lie is selfish, when the deceit is unauthorised, when the liar is ill-practised and when the liar and his or her target are similar in terms of personality and social values.

● fear about being caught (detection apprehension): the more serious the threatened consequences of the lie, the more nervous the liar. Detection apprehension occurs most strongly when the target has a reputation for being suspicious and difficult to fool, when the stakes are high in terms of rewards and punishment, when the liar is less practised or has been an unsuccessful liar in the past and when the target benefits little from the lie.

● duping delight (relief after the lie): the observable and puzzling relief shown after a lie has been told. A person is caught for duping delight most often when the target of the lie poses a challenge because he or she has a reputation for being difficult to fool. It also occurs when others are watching or can appreciate the skilful performance of the liar.

Extensive and very careful research by experts in the area has revealed that betrayal of concealed information is organised by the type of information. Indirect speech, pauses, speech errors and decreased illustrators indicate that the verbal lie is not prepared. Slips of the tongue, tirades, micro-expression or squelched expression often indicate powerful emotion. Blushing, gazing down or away means embarrassment, while decreased illustrators, and slower and softer speech can mean boredom.

Clues that an expression is false include absence of reliable forehead expression and showing fear or sadness. A smile is not really a happy smile if your eye muscles are not involved. If illustrators fail to increase or the timing of illustrators is incorrect it shows that a person is not as enthusiastic or involved as he or she may pretend. Absence of sweating, changed respiration or increased manipulators (self-touching) can mean that a person is not having the negative emotions of fear or anger he or she is pretending to.

## Catching liars (detecting possible indicators of dissimulation)

There are some simple but important points to bear in mind when trying to catch liars:

● Establish base-rate behaviour. What are they like when they are normal, relaxed and telling the truth? Give people time to relax and see what they are like when it is unlikely they are lying. Some people fidget more than others. Neurotics are more anxious than the stable most of the time. There are numerous idiosyncratic but stable non-verbal behavioural differences between individuals. It is too easy to mistake particular signs such as sweating or avoiding eye gaze as a betrayal of anxiety and a function of lying when it is perfectly normal everyday behaviour for that person.

■ Look for sudden changes in verbal, vocal or visual behaviour such as movements. It is when behaviour noticeably alters that it is most meaningful.

▲ Note any mismatch between what is being said and how it is being said as well as any differences in anxiety level as certain topics are raised. When the eyes, the voice and the words spoken are not in emotional synchrony, it may well be a very good sign of lying. A forced smile or laugh to accompany the carefully prepared verbal line can be a powerful indicator that 'something interesting is going on'.

● Formulate a hypothesis as to the cause: what are they lying about, what is the sensitive issue? Not everything is a lie. Why should they be lying about some issues and not others?

● Test the theory by bringing up a particular topic (the area of the lies) and see if the non-verbal pattern re-occurs. If there are persistent indicators of discomfort when particular topics are reintroduced into the conversation, one may assume a stronger possibility of lying.

The bottom line, however, is that for even the trained expert it is often very difficult to detect liars. We have video-tapes of famous spies lying; of murderers who pretend to be victims appealing for help; of politicians telling bare-faced lies in video close-ups. They succeed in fooling hundreds of people.

Even the lie-detector can be relatively easily fooled. Studies using it have shown that when misdiagnosis occurs it is much more likely that an innocent person is judged guilty than the other way around.

So beware the person who claims to be good at spotting liars in the interview. It could be true – or a self-delusional porkie!

# bibliography and further reading

The following books were consulted in preparing this one. Those marked with an asterisk are recommended to the reader as useful, more detailed sources for further reading.

* ARGYLE M. (1994) *Bodily Communication*. London, Routledge.

BENTHAL J. *and* POLKEMUS T. (eds) (1975) *The Body as a Medium of Communication*. London, Allen Lane.

COLLETT P. (1994) *Foreign Bodies: A guide to European mannerisms*. London, Simon and Schuster.

* EKMAN P. (1976) *Telling Lies*. New York, Berkeley.

EKMAN P. *and* FRIESEN W. (1972) 'Hand movements'. *Journal of Communication*. Vol. 22. pp253-374.

FAST J. (1980) *Body Language*. London, Pan.

GOLEMAN D. (1995) *Emotional Intelligence*. New York, Bantam Books.

LYLE J. (1997) *Understanding Body Language*. London, Chancellor Press.

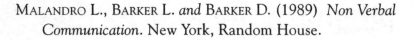

MALANDRO L., BARKER L. *and* BARKER D. (1989)  *Non Verbal Communication*. New York, Random House.

* MORRIS D. (1982)  *Manwatching: A guide to human behaviour*. London, Granada.

MORRIS D., COLLETT P., MARSH P. *and* O'SHAUGHNESSEY M. (1979)  *Gestures: Their origin and distribution*. London, Johnathan Cape.

* PEASE A. (1990)  *Body Language: How to read others' thoughts by their gestures*. London, Sheldon Press.

With over 100,000 members, the **Chartered Institute of Personnel and Development** is the largest organisation in Europe dealing with the management and development of people. The CIPD operates its own publishing unit, producing books and research reports for human resource practitioners, students, and general managers charged with people management responsibilities.

Currently there are over 160 titles covering the full range of personnel and development issues. The books have been commissioned from leading experts in the field and are packed with the latest information and guidance to best practice.

For free copies of the CIPD Books Catalogue, please contact the publishing department:

Tel.: 020 8263 3387
Fax: 020 8263 3850
E-mail: publish@cipd.co.uk
Web: www.cipd.co.uk/publications

Orders for books should be sent to:

Plymbridge Distributors
Estover
Plymouth
Devon
PL6 7PZ

(Credit card orders) Tel.: 01752 202 301
Fax: 01752 202 333

Other titles in the *Management Shapers* series

*All titles are priced at £5.95 (£5.36 to IPD members)*

## The Appraisal Discussion

Terry Gillen

Shows you how to make appraisal a productive and motivating experience for all levels of performer. It includes:

- assessing performance fairly and accurately

- using feedback to improve performance

- handling reluctant appraisees and avoiding bias

- agreeing future objectives

- identifying development needs.

1998  96 pages    0 85292 751 7

## Assertiveness

Terry Gillen

Will help you feel naturally confident, enjoy the respect of others and easily establish productive working relationships, even with 'awkward' people. It covers:

- understanding why you behave as you do and, when that behaviour is counter-productive, knowing what to do about it

- understanding other people better

- keeping your emotions under control

- preventing others' bullying, flattering or manipulating you

- acquiring easy-to-learn techniques that you can use immediately

- developing your personal assertiveness strategy.

1998  96 pages     0 85292 769 X

## Constructive Feedback

### Roland and Frances Bee

Practical advice on when to give feedback, how best to give it, and how to receive and use feedback yourself. It includes:

- using feedback in coaching, training, and team motivation

- distinguishing between criticism and feedback

- 10 tools of giving constructive feedback

- dealing with challenging situations and people.

1998  96 pages    0 85292 752 5

## The Disciplinary Interview

Alan Fowler

This book will ensure that you adopt the correct procedures, conduct productive interviews and manage the outcome with confidence. It includes:

- understanding the legal implications

- investigating the facts and presenting the management case

- probing the employee's case and diffusing conflict

- distinguishing between conduct and competence

- weighing up the alternatives to dismissal.

1998  96 pages    0 85292 753 3

## Leadership Skills

John Adair

*Leadership Skills* will give you confidence, guidance and inspiration as you journey from being an effective manager to becoming a leader of excellence. Acknowledged as a world authority on leadership, Adair offers stimulating insights on:

- recognising and developing your leadership qualities

- acquiring the personal authority to give positive direction and the flexibility to embrace change

- acting on the key interacting needs – to achieve your task, build your team and develop its members

- transforming such core leadership functions such as planning, communicating and motivating into practical skills that you can master.

1998 96 pages     0 85292 764 9